MALAYSIAN COOKBOOK

2

SUSAN SAM

TABLE OF CONTENTS

Green Veggie Sambal Rice

Super Easy Satay Sauce

My Lovely Tasty Creamy Curried Poultry With Spinach

Kerrie Noedelslaai / Curry Noodle Salad

Laksa Spicy Tuna Pasta

Authentic Malaysian Style Vegetable Curry

Chai Tow Kway - Radish Cake

Mee Siam

Seri Muka (Malay Ethnic Cuisine)

Pan Mee Soup

Roti Canai

Batik Cake

Assam Pedas Chicken

Kek Batik / Marie Biscuits Cake - NO BAKE

Pumpkin And Coconut Kuih Talam

Kuih Lopes (Coconut Glutinous Rice)

Baked Spicy Stingray / Sambal Ikan Bakar

Fifteen Minute LAKSA

INTRODUCTION

Malaysian cuisine includes planning food traditions and methods found in Malaysia, and shows the multi-ethnic makeup of its inhabitants. Almost all Malaysia's inhabitants can roughly be divided among 3 major ethnic groupings: Malays, Chinese and Indians.

Since Peninsular Malaysia stocks and shares a common history with Singapore, pretty to find variants of the same dish across both sides of the border regardless of the host to origin, such as laksa and chicken rice. Malaysia stocks and shares culinary ties with Indonesia, Thailand and the Philippines, as they nations often share certain foods, such as satay and rendang.

1. Rojak – Malaysian Spicy Fruit Salad

Ingredients

6 small deep fried tofu
½ pineapple (peeled and cut into chunks)
1 green mango (peeled and cubed)
1 small jicama (peeled and cubed)
one small cucumber (cut into bite size pieces)
¼ cup peanuts (toasted and chopped)
1 tbsp sesame seeds (toasted)
Rojak Sauce
1 tbsp sambal belacan
1 tbsp hoisin sauce or sweet sauce
1 tbsp sweet soy sauce
1 tbsp sweet black shrimp paste
2 tbsp sugar

Directions

Smolder tofu on a non-stick pan upon all sides to crisp it up. Remove and cut thinly when amazing enough to offer with. Arranged apart.

Combine most rojak sauce elements in a little dish. Mix completely with a tea tea spoon.

Place sliced tofu, pineapple, mango, jicama, and cucumber in the large dish.

Put sauce more than vegetables and fruits. Mix well.

Dish into 4 individual portions. Sprinkle some chopped nut products and sesame seeds products over every part.

Serve instantly.

2. Easy Rojak Recipe

Ingredients

8 tbsp sugar
1 tsp Salt
1 tbsp lime zest
1 whole lime
2 tbsp chilli prawn
1 tsp shrimp paste
4 tbsp tamarind paste
6 tbsp roasted peanuts chopped coarsely
1/2 cup lime juice
1 whole lime
2 1/4 cup pineapples sliced or chunks
180 g cucumbers sliced
200 g jicama peeled and sliced
One hundred and sixty g tofu puffs Fried tofu is a good substitute
227 g cuttlefish balls thawed if frozen

Directions

In a very very 375F oven, toasted bread tofu puffs till crispy intended meant for a couple of minutes. Set apart. Cut the tofu puffs by 50 % using scissors.
Cut cucumbers.
Peel off jicama and cut in to pieces. Thick or slim is your choice. Thick intended meant for some crunchiness; slender for melt in your mouth persistence.
In a large bowl, add sugar, salt, crispy prawn chilli, sauteed shrimp paste, tamarind put, lime zest and lime juice and stir.
Roughly cut some peanuts. Add 4 tbsp of roasted peanuts in to the spices.
When the frosty cuttlefish balls have got thawed, pan smolder till golden meant for eight to a few momemts.
Add the cuttlefish golf balls towards the spices. In the event that using discontinued pineapple, drain the juice. (Save the juice to make a smoothie later)
Add cucumbers, jicama, pineapple towards the dish. Utilize a wood spoon to mix well.
Just before providing, add the done tofu puffs. Blend well till spices coats the constituents.

Add one more two tbsp sliced nuts (or more because you like) because toppings.

3. Malaysian Sago Sweet (Sabudana Ki Methai)

Ingredients

1 cup Sago
1 cup Sugar
1 1/2 cups Fresh grated coconut
salt little

Directions

Consider 1 cup sago /sabudana and 1 cup blood glucose.

Maintain fresh grated coconut ready. Saturate sabudana for an hour or so or so. There after take 4 cups of water and a single glass glucose and maintain this on gas. Enable sugar to melt and steam.

Steam this sabudana obtain cooked and makes smooth determination.

Add color to it and pour it in to a dish and invite this to arrive to room heat range.

Take little spend spoon make this for the plate with grated coconut added with pinch of sodium in this. Move this blend upon the grated coconut and place this within a dish.

Refrigerate this golf balls pertaining to sometime and provide it cool.

4. Spicy Malaysian Shrimp & Snowpeas

Ingredients

1 lb raw shrimp, deveined and peeled
1 1/2 cup snowpeas
3 clove garlic, minced
1 1/2 tbsp fresh ginger, minced
2 tbsp Red curry paste
1/2 cup low sodium chicken stock
1 lime, zest and juice
1 tbsp sesame oil

Marinade
1/4 cup soya sauce
3/4 tbsp cornstarch
four tbsp whisky (or chicken stock if you don't cook with alcohol)

Directions

Combine ingredients for vinaigrette and marinade shrimp for 30 a few momemts.

High temperature oil in wok/pan, and mix smolder garlic, ginger and red curry insert.

Add shrimp to wok, and add 2 the the majority of effective spinner's from the dressing as well. Cook till shrimp just convert red (but still raw-ish).

Add your snow peas along with your chicken discuss. Cook until shrimp fully cooked and Snowpeas cooked yet nevertheless crisp.

Complete with all the " lemon inch juice and passion and serve with steamed grain or noodles.

5. Talam Pandan (Malaysian Dessert)

Ingredients

Green pandan layer
150 g rice flour
50 g green pea flour
230 g sugar
Eight hundred 15 (screwpine) Pandan juice from
pandan leaves liters
1 tsp water alkaline
200 ml Coconut cream layer
600 ml water santan
60 g rice flour
60 g green pea flour
3 g salt

Directions

Green Pandan (Bottom Layer):
Incorporate all the dried out ingredients in a bowl and mix in the pandan juice. Tension mixture proper saucepan and cook more than low warmth till mixture somewhat thickens. Remove through the temperature.
Put mixture in to an 8in greased mould and vapour for about 20-25 minutes till founded.
Coconut Layer (Top Layer):
Combine every single the dry substances within a dish. Stir in coconut milk and consuming water.
Cook more than low heat till blend thickens regarding almost eight moments.
Remove from warmth and put coconut layer on to the green pandan layer.
Steam regarding another a quarter-hour.
Remove from machine and let this cool for in least four hours just before cutting.

6. Popiah (Malaysian Spring Roll)

Ingredients

one turnip large , grated (also known as jicama)
two bean curd pieces of , diced into small pieces
one hundred and fifty g prawns medium shelled
(diced into small pieces)
3 eggs
5 cloves garlic , chopped finely
shallots Fried
lettuce leaves Fresh , clean and drained dried out

turnip Seasoning for filling :
1 tsp soy sauce
1/2 tsp white pepper powder
1/2 tsp sugar
1 cup water

Sauces :
1/2 cup Hoisin sauce sauce or sweet
1/4 cup sambal chili sauce (Chili paste)

Directions

Within a wok, temperature essential oil on moderate fireplace, and smolder two cloves of sliced garlic till aromatic, and after that include grated turnip. Add soy spices or herbs, sugar and pepper for seasoning. Combine fry for the first 5 minutes.

Add water and minimize heat to low, cover and leave the turnip to cook related to another 30 -- 40 minutes until soft. Add more soy sauce and sugar if necessary. When cooked, tension the juice in to a small pot and maintain warm. The juice may be accepted since a gravy in the popiah.

While the turnip is meals preparation, heat essential oil in a individual wok, add one particular clove of sliced garlic clove and deep-fry the veggie curd till gently browned. Dish away and drain any kind of liquid.

With the same wok, put more oil and heat. Add in those various various other chopped garlic, and when fried, contain the prawns. Offer a dash of soy bean spices, white pepper & oyster spices. Mix fry the prawns until prepared. Provide away.

Defeat the eggs and smolder them omelette-style in the same wok. Then cut in to thin shreds.

Place aside every completing individual bowls or tiffin.

Lay an item of the popiah wrapper on the dish and spread one particular teaspoon of hoisin sauce and 1/2 teaspoon of sambal throughout the middle.

Place person in the lettuce family leaf within the gravies.

Spoon 2-3 tablespoons in the strained turnip filling onto the leaf.

In levels, best with deep-fried veggie curd, prawn, crab meat, sliced up egg omelette and deep-fried shallot crisps.

Collapse the edges in the wrapper, stay in firmly and roll-up tight. Cut into three to four parts.

Put a tea tea spoon from the turnip juice within the popiah. Serve & DEVOUR immediately.

7. Sambal (Malaysian Chili Pepper Sauce)

Ingredients

250 grams Sambal paste
3 tbsp Vegetable oil
5 tbsp Sugar
1 tbsp Salt

Directions

Warmness oil in a pot or wok, add the sambal paste, and sauté well. If you don't sauté the mixture well enough, it is going to give you a tummy pain. Heat over moderate.

Add the sugar and salt and continue to sauté. When cooled, this is going to harden a small bit. Keep close track of this and if this appears too company, add some drinking water. Be it thoroughly combined, it's done.

In the event that you add deep-fried anchovies and deep-fried peanuts, it is usually going to become the Malaysian dish called "Sambal Ikan Bilis. "

8. Bubur Kacang Hijau- Malaysian Sweet Green Veggie Soup

Ingredients

200 grams Mung beans (Green Beans)
3 Pandan leaves
one as much (to taste) Palm sugar or brown sugar
1 as much (to taste) Caster sugar
1 pinch Salt
200 ml Coconut milk

Directions

This is really a pandan woods (called screw pinus radiata in English). In the event that you possibly can easily get dried out leaves, utilize them; or else, you may create your personal.
Just in case you probably could get new pandan leaves, clean them well, after that connect them in a knot. In the event that they are really dried out, use them becoming.

Rinse the mung beans and place these questions container with drinking drinking water. Provide for a boil, then drain (to remove the scum).

Return the beans to the pot and add the pandan leaves. Fill the box with lots of water and vapor until the coffee beans are soft. We use a pressure cooker with this step.

When the beans are smooth, get rid of the pandan leaves. Then add the palm sugar, white-colored sugar, and salt to taste.

Add the coconut dairy products and mix well. In relation to a steam, it can done.

Mung coffee beans have a chilling effect on the body. Using chilly soup to cool-down is a great way to conserve energy!

For research, this is the percentage of elements that I consider benefit of to make this: three hundred g mung coffee beans, two hundred and fifty g caster sugars, 50 g brownish sugar, and two hundred ml coconut dairy. It can a lttle little bit on the fairly sweet part.

9. Sambal Telur (Malaysian-Style Hard Boiled Eggs In Chili Sauce)

Ingredients

6 Eggs
1/2 large Onion
5 tbsp Sambal paste
2 tbsp Tamarind paste
3 tbsp Sugar
1 rounded teaspoon Salt
1 Vegetable oil

Directions

Make hard-boiled eggs and peel the addresses. Cut the onions horizontally into five mm thick parts.
This is tamarind paste and the package it appeared in. It's a great alkali element. Launched too hard to obtain, that may be possible to replacement with soft umeboshi (pickled plum).
Add water for the tamarind paste and dissolve the put with your convenience. It is feasible to only make use of the strained water. Once you utilize the liquid, replicate with additional water in least twice.
Temperature veggie oil in a very very skillet and sauté the onions. Once they will are soft, add the sambal insert and continue sautéing. If this begins to scorch, add water.
Sauté well and add the tamarind water from Third step since well as the boiled ovum. Period with sugars and salt, and simmer until the water evaporates.
You might use poulet ovum rather than poultry eggs. Fried tofu certainly is the great substitute.

10. Cassava Cake (Malaysian Binka Ubi)

Ingredients

1 lb cassava/yucca root
1 1/4 cup dark brown sugar
1/2 stick butter (melted)
1 egg (slightly beaten)
200 ml coconut milk
1 pinch salt

Directions

Pre-specified the oven 375°F.

Peel off and grate cassava. The one I truly bought was 1) 37 lb. Right after it should become around 1lb.

Important!!! many people white-colored, which often is usually bitter, they possess far better press the juice aside and replace this with the comparison water. I bought an entire underlying and grated this, yet some quality recipes I actually noticed mention regarding freezing cassava. Can attempt it the following time, probably it will probably be less complicated to grate..

Combine elements.

11. Valentines Gift Cake

Ingredients

For base
Dry ingredients
1 cup all-purpose flour
1/4 cup Malaysian cocoa powder
1/4 cup cocoa powder
1/2 teaspoon baking powder
1/4 teaspoon baking soda
1 teaspoon instant coffee powder
1/4 teaspoon salt
Wet ingredients
1/2 cup odour less oil
3/4 cup buttermilk
1 cup powdered sugar
1/2 teaspoon vanilla extract

For frosting
50 gm white chocolate
2 tablespoon strawberry crush
as needed Red gel food colour

1 1/2 cup sweetened ready nondairy whipped cream
as needed blue gel colour
handful colorful and silver sprinklers

Directions

Meant for base, sieve virtually all dry ingredients with each other in a dish.

In another dish, add oil and buttermilk. Mix this. After that add powder glucose to this. Combine it till glucose dissolves. After that add vanilla pull out in this.

Right now in wet combination add the dried away mixture. And mix it by cut and fold technique. Dont overmix this. Just mix this till the straightforward uniformity. Meanwhile preset the the oven in 170° for 10 minutes.

Take middle shape cake form. Apply some gas and butter paper on the bottom level level. Add dessert mixture in to the mould. And preserve it in the oven and cook for around 25-30 minutes. Look for guidance from toothpick in the event comes crystal clear there after cake can be cooked. So bottom is normally ready.

After aiming to cool aside completely. Unmould this. Eliminate the butter paper. Cut upper dried out coating to make a smooth surface area. After that cut the wedding wedding ceremony ceremony cake out of your middle. Using electric powered beater defeat the whipped cream till to get nondroping uniformity. Apply this whipped cream around the one element of dessert after applying cover this to component.

Now apply whipped cream uniformly every around the dessert and make a simple area. Inside a remaining cream add 3 to 4 drops of reddish food color. Fill it in the piping handbag and create edge and beautiful styles from the choice throughout the dessert.

For red and red minds, micro wave white chocolates for virtually any minute. Add blood crush into dissolved chocolate. And fill up this in the heart formed silicon mould. Refrigerator this for five to ten minutes and unmould the minds. Intended for reddish colored hearts add reddish colored food color on the dissolved chocolate. And fill it in the mould. Beautify the cake with these kinds of hearts.

And gorgeous and super delicious heart shaped Valentine day cake can be prepared.

12. My Leftover Lamb Curry

Ingredients

1/2 onion died
1 tbls Butter
1/2 tsp Garlic granuals
1/2 tsp Cracked Black pepper
4 Cups chopped leftover cooked lamb
1/2 Cup Frozen peas

curry sauce
four tbls the malaysian curry and 0.25 cup cold
water
3 cups boiling water

Directions

Melt the Butter in a very very non stay baking pan. After that add the diced onions, garlic and pepper mix in fry for 1 minutes.

Next add the Chop up lamb and mix then add the peas.

Pour inside the lamb drinking water and mix.

Following add the mounds of curry to a combining dish and add the cold drinking drinking water whisk until easy.

Next add the curry paste in the direction of the lamb mix and stir until all mixed and thick. Allow this to simmer designed for a few of minutes.

Add to a offering bowl and provide hot with grain or potato potato chips.

13. Green Veggie Sambal Rice

Ingredients

3 tablespoons Malaysian Sambal Paste
1 cup cooked rice
1 head broccoli
1 handful spring onions
1 handful green beans
1 handful bean sprouts
1 handful peas
1 tablespoon cooking oil
1 teaspoon sesame oil
1 tablespoon soy sauce
1 tablespoon sweet soy sauce

Directions

Vapour the veg related to some minutes.
Temperatures the cooking gas on high therefore when it's well-known add the great rice.
Fry the rice for a few minutes and add the vegetables
Add the sambal paste and combine through. Add the sesame seed gas, soy sauce and sweet soy sauce. when it's piping well-known, it's ready. I actually really served after some extra sambal paste since this is so delicious!

14. Super Easy Satay Sauce

Ingredients

one jar crunchy peanut butter (approx 400g)
one tin coconut cream 400ml
one tablespoon red curry paste (I use Malaysian one here)
one teaspoon crushed garlic
one Tablespoon soy sauce
one tablespoon sweet chilli sauce

Directions

Destroy all ingredients together, Adjust spice, sodium and sweet with chilli, soy bean sauce, and sugar.
Warm through in saucepan.

15. My Lovely Tasty Creamy Curried Poultry With Spinach

Ingredients

1 tbls Olive oil
1 large onion chopped small
1 tsp Grated Ginger
2 Crushed Garlic cloves
3 Chicken breast cut into 1 inch cubes
3-4 Curry leaves
1/2 tsp Corriander
1/2 tsp Salt
1/2 tsp Black Pepper
1/2 tsp Cumin
1/2 tsp Chilli powder
1 tsp Garam Masala
1 pint Boiling water
1/2 Fresh Green chilli chopped (about 1 tsp full)
1 Tbls Malaysian curry paste
2 chicken stock cubes
2 handful Baby Spinach
1/2 Cup Double cream

Directions

Warm-up the oil. Have the ability to the first 9 spices or herbal products ready and add one after one more quickly and a quick mix after that add boil eating water.

So Preliminary Add the onions and fry to get a moment.

Then the ginger and garlic clove clove fry pertaining to 30 secounds and combine into the onions.

Add the poultry and mix it in after that add the following 7 spices upon checklist pursuing the chicken stir quick and fry for 1 minute.

Then add the boiling consuming water let this bubble for 1 minute stirring.

Following add the two poultry stock cubes combine in the poultry and combine.

Add the malaysian curry paste to a little cool drinking water combine and add this on the chicken curry. Mix when this comes to the steam turn this down and simmer.

Add the hadfuls of spinach and rip it and drop in and mix. Leave pertaining to the rest of the cooking period on low.

After the 30 minutes take it away the warmth and let it great for about five minutes.

Add the Cream and the Lemon juice mix and mix well. It will eventually go a lovely yellow color.

Place it back again on the temperature and warm this up slowly upon medium until acquiring into consideration the steam then change it down and prepare slow pertaining to a couple of minutes.

Serve with Grain long wheat or Basmatti.

16. Kerrie Noedelslaai / Curry Noodle Salad

Ingredients

500 g Noodles
1 Tablespoon Hot Curry Powder
1 Tablespoon Malaysian Curry Powder
1 Tablespoon Turmeric Ground
two Tea Spoons Black Pepper and Salt to taste
1 Cup Tomato Sauce
1/2 Cup Brown Vinegar
1/2 Cup Vegitable Oil
200 g Sugar
two Tea Spoons medium ground Black Pepper and Salt to taste
1 Green Pepper / Capsicum
1 Large onion

Directions

Vapor the noodles make use of a little of petrol and sodium in the drinking water.
Cut the red onion and Green / Reddish Pepper carefully.
Make the Spices blend the tomato spices, vinigar, essential oil and sugar jointly blend well.
Stress the Noodles established up mixing dish add the onions and Peppers.
Mix the sauce in and add Dark Pepper and Sodium.
Refrigerate over evening time.

17. Laksa Spicy Tuna Pasta

Ingredients

Angel hair pasta

Paste
1 tbsp chopped garlic
1 clove shallot
1 tbsp chopped ginger
1 tbsp chopped lemongrass
Canned chili tuna
80 ml Coconut milk

Garnish
Limes
Chopped Laksa leave

Directions

Vapor pasta to e dante, or pre al dante. Nudeln will be overcook later.

Mix many the paste with each other. Make use of mortar and bother if any kind of. Fry all of them.

Add one entire may of hot and spicy tuna with soup and a little bit of the important petrol.

Add teigwaren inside. Blend.

Add coconut milk. Combine. Change off high temperature.

Add laksa keep and lime to ornament.

18. Authentic Malaysian Style Vegetable Curry

Ingredients

4 tbsp Vegetable oil (safflower or canola)
1/2 Red onion
20 Shallots
10 clove Garlic
2 stalks Lemongrass (cut into fourths)
6 Cloves
1 piece Star anise
1 Cinnamon stick
10 Okra
1 Bitter gourd
1 Eggplant (slim Japanese type)
1 one packet Atsuage
5 Satsuma-age
1/2 Onion (sliced)
ten tbsp Curry powder (preferably imported from Malaysia or Singapore)
5 Pandan leaves (optional)

Directions

Combine all of the 1-3 ingredients in a food processor chip chip and heartbeat to a paste-like uniformity.

Grease a container with essential oil, and heat the insert from The first step. Once cooked through, add the four - 7 substances and stir-fry till the moisture evaporates, and also the insert is decreased by 1/2 the original amount.

To get ready the bitter gourd, cut it by 50 % lengthwise, completely scoop out the pith utilizing a tea spoon, then cut this into 8-mm heavy rounds.

Cut the onion into heavy slices.

Cut the okra by 50 %, and approximately chop the eggplant into pieces (then soak in water). Cut the atsuage and satsuma-age into similarly size pieces. Sizes could finish up being random.

Add the constituents prepared in Steps 3-5 towards the whole container, and stir-fry. After the ingredients are prepared through, add the curry powdered. Prepare while stir-frying. Add enough drinking water to protect the elements, from then on simmer for 20-30 minutes.

To get people who are certainly not really on the diet program plan, add coconut dairy to taste (but do not allow it boil after adding).

For individuals for the diet program program, in the event that you like a more potent taste, add a little of evaporated dairy or milk.

In the event that offered, add pandan leaves in Stage almost eight.

In the event that preparing vegetarian style, omit the satsuma-age.

19. Chai Tow Kway - Radish Cake

Ingredients

1 radish
2 stalks Green chives
Shallot
Dark soy sauce
Oyster sauce
Dried shrimp
1 cup beansprouts
Flour

Directions

Grate radish and enable it to vapor for five. moments. Remove and clean with water after that set aside. Subsequent pound the dried out out shrimps in to small pieces. Blend it with grated radish. In a little dish place a littoe drinking water and one tbsp flour. Put once again in. the grated radish. Blend most properly. After that let it prepare for five moments. When done remove and place apart. until. it obtain cool. Then maintain in the refrigerator to chill to get 2 hours.

After two hour remove from your fridge and cut intol cubes.

Heat wok add oil then blend fry shallots till soft. Then add radish cubeband smolder a. small little bit then add green chives and. beansprout. Season with oyster spices and dark soy bean spices. Chilli spices the optional.

20. Mee Siam

Ingredients

Three hundred g rice vermicelli (meehoon) - soak in water for 5 minutes and drain
300 g prawns - peel and devein
one cup beansprouts (peel both ends to get a crunchier bite texture)
1 cup chives, cut into 3 cm length
0.25 cup dried shrimps, wash and chopped coarsely
2 pcs firm tofu, slices (optional
4 kaffir lime leaves, shredded finely
1/3 cup cooking oil
Calamsansi cut in halves to serve on the side (optional)

Ingredients to be pounded or blended together:
4 cloves garlic
4 shallots
1 1/2 tsp turmeric powder
3 Tbsp chopped ginger flower (Bunga Kantan)
1 stalk lemongrass chopped finely
three bird eye chilies (if you like it spicy)

Seasonsings:
2 Tbsp fish sauce
1 Tbsp soy sauce
1/2 Tbsp tamarind paste
2 tsp sugar
1 tsp chicken stock granules
1/2 tsp white pepper
2 cups water

Directions

Prepare all the components!

Heat oil in the wok. Softly fry the dried out out shrimps and tofu but individually. Dish out make apart.

Stir smolder the pounded elements and kaffir lime green leaves until fragrant. Add prawns and smolder until they will may be half-cooked. Dish out the particular prawns and place aside.

Add in seasonings and supply to boil. Next add meehoon and stir-fry.

Mix in dried shrimps, tofu, prawns, chives and beansprouts. Mix almost all of them well for a couple of minutes or until everything are ready. Provide with cut lime green at the aspect to drizzle in the event that preferred.

21. Seri Muka (Malay Ethnic Cuisine)

Ingredients

Glutinous Rice
500 g rice soaked overnight
500 ml coconut milk
to taste Salt

Pandan Layer
150 ml Pandan Juice
150 g sugar
3 large eggs
100 g wheat flour
400 ml coconut milk
to taste Salt

Directions

Drain the rice, place it in a cake baking holder or any type that has the similar depth. Add one pandan leaf. Mix the coconut dairy with salt and add to the rice. The coconut milk must be very slightly inside the rice. As a result watch it when you pour. Place it in the steamer for 25 mins or until it's ready
Today when the grain is definitely prepared stir well, obtain rid of the pandan leaf and press compactly inside the baking type. This really is definitely really to guarantee whenever we place the pandan covering it does not really really slip through the grain.
To get the pandan coating. Add all of the ingriedients and pulse inside a blender. Together with a machine, stir the mix until it actually is definitely thicker. Then put inside the sizzling grain. Steam an extra half an hour.
Cool it directly down before you might cut. Consume inside twenty 4 hours because it will definitely go bad quickly. You might store in the refrigerator nevertheless the materials can become hard.

22. Pan Mee Soup

Ingredients

500 g minced meat
1/2 cup minced garlic
0.25 cup dried chilies, sliced or chopped (if using flakes, try to find some with less seeds and more chili pieces)
1/2 cup minced onion
0.5 cup sliced shiitake mushrooms (preferably dried & soaked overnight. Reserve soaking liquid)
0.5 cup dried anchovies (I prefer to grind up the anchovies using a food processor. In the event that not available, you can replace this with some deep-fried bacon. Please adjust salt content accordingly)
two cups pucuk manis (can be substituted with baby/round spinach)
2 anchovy/fish bouillon cubes
1/4 cup vegetable oil
To taste soy sauce
To taste salt
To taste white pepper
To taste sugar

Optional: eggs/tofu
Egg/rice noodles

Directions

Temperature 2-3 tbsp in the oil in a soup container.
Mix fry 2 tbsp of garlic clove till fragrant then add
the minced meats and 1/2 the anchovies. Sauté till
cooked then add the mushrooms. Prepare for 5-6 a
few momemts until the meat is slightly browned.
Season well with soy bean sauce and white color
pepper. You can a quantity of tablespoons of
water/the soaking water in the mushrooms if this
gets too dried up. Remove all yet 0.25 cup of the
mixture make apart.

In the whole container with all of those other zero.
25 cup from the mixture, add the bouillon cubes & 6
mugs of water (you actually might also make use of
the mushroom soaking water & top up drinking
water to get six cups). Encourage the water to arrive
to a steam and add spinach / pucuk manis. Cook for
several minutes until the colour changes to a more
dark green, then change away heat and season the
soups.

Within a person pan, heat the remaining oil. This truly is okay if this seems like a great deal. Once popular, sauté onions and leftover anchovies and garlic clove until browned and slightly crispy. Add chili and sauté for several minutes. Be prepared for the soup to generate you hacking and coughing! Season beside soy bean sauce/salt/white pepper and sugar, if preferred.

To provide SOUPS VERSION: it is possible to possibly boil all the noodles inside a separate box and eat every immediately or tea spoon a few of the soup in to a individual lesser pot and steam them in person servings. Steam the noodles in the soup and add an egg/some tofu to poach in when the noodles are almost performed. Ladle the minced meat/chili on best as preferred.

To serve DRY release: boil the noodles separately so when cooked, immediately mix with the toppings - minced meat & chili. This is possible to poach an egg and add this at the very top.

23. Roti Canai

Ingredients

3 cups multi-purpose flour
2 tablespoons ghee/butter
1 tablespoon condensed milk
1 teaspoon salt
2 teaspoons sugar
1/2 teaspoon baking soda
1 egg
1/4 cup water

Directions

MAKING THE DOUGH... Stroke all the components proper dough, adding water in in the end.
When the dough does not stay to your requirements needs hands, rub for five to ten minutes, then cover with cling film and rest meant for 15 mins.
Rub an additional five to ten mins. After that cover with cling film and loosen up for at least 30 minutes.
Important oil a pot with melted ghee or cooking essential oil.

Separate the money in to tennis balls the sizes of golf tennis tennis balls. Soak them in melted ghee/oil in the container to get at least eight hours, protected in the refrigerator.

FLICKING & BAKING THE ROTI... Essential oil the table/counter.

Trim and slap regarding money ball. Spread this evenly obtainable, after that possibly flip (lift up and toss down) or press this within the counter until it truly is definitely stretched out and semi-transparent.

Add blended ghee/oil onto the stretched dough, and also any filling you'the like to place in this (eg, egg, parmesan cheese, plums, etc). After that possibly fold this in to a square or move it in a rose.

Launched a rose, press away into a toned circle prior to frying.

Move this within a pre-heated and oiled skillet. Smolder both edges until parts of it switch fantastic brown. Filler in the roti simply by clapping this through the sides.

Offer hot with dhal or curry.

24. Batik Cake

Ingredients

For the cake
2 packs digestive biscuits
200 g butter
1/2 cup condensed milk
1/2 cup cocoa powder
1 cup chocolate-flavored malt powder
1/2 cup hot water
1/2 tsp salt
1 egg
1 tsp vanilla essence

For the Choc ganache
200 g whipped cream
200 g dark choc
1 tbsp butter
1 tsp vanilla essence

Directions

Inside a huge dish, break the cookies into 4 items, each. And place it aside.

In a pan, warmth the butter on medium low warmth. Add the cacao natural powder, the malt powdered, compacted milk, sodium, hot water, egg and vanilla substance. Mix occasionally till all the blend is melted. After that, get rid of the blend from heat. Add the cookies and blend this until the chocolates sauce is well coupled with cookies. Then transfer the biscuit blend in to a round cooking skillet. Press the most effective till the surface is usually flat and relax it in the refrigerator.

For the chocolate ganache, within a bowl, break the dark chocolates pub into little items. Then, warmth the whipped cream within a skillet. To be able to starts to steam, change off temperature and pour the cream into the dish of chocolates. Maintain stirring until the chocolate is dissolved. Add the butter and vanilla substance and mix till everything is well mixed.

Put the chocolate ganache in to the biscuits combination, and chilled this in the refrigerator.

25. Assam Pedas Chicken

Ingredients

Main Ingredient
Half Chicken
2 Red Onion
2 Garlic
1/3 finger Ginger
3 Candle Nuts
15 Dried Chillies
2/3 finger Shrimp Paste
1/2 tsp Turmeric Powder
1 tbsp Black Pepper
Tamarind Paste

For Tasting
Leaves Laksa
Salt

Directions

Marinate chicken with salt and turmeric powder. Fry till 50 % done.

Cut dried up chillies, put in hot water. Clean and cut reddish colored onion, garlic cloves, ginger. Put every little thing in the meals blender, add abit of water, turmeric powdered and also the shrimp insert. Mix till this turns into a paste.

Warmth up the petrol in medium warmth in the preparing meals pan. Include the blended and sautee till aromatic.

Tamarind paste blend with water and arranged in the skillet. Set up a few drinking water little bit by little little bit. Then place in the half cooled down off chicken. Combined well, salt and laksa leaves to become added in together. From then on simmer in low warmth.

Finish up simply by serving with white-colored rice, gravy within the best with most the poultry.

26. Kek Batik / Marie Biscuits Cake - NO BAKE

Ingredients

1 row Marie Biscuits
1/2 can sweetened condensed milk
4 tbsp cocoa powder / chocolate powder
100 gm butter / margarine

Directions

Break down butter on low heat. Add compressed milk and cacao powder. Mix well.
Add crushed deal biscuits and blend well. Turn away heat.
Lay in preferred baking frying pan make to awesome in fridge more than night.

27. Pumpkin And Coconut Kuih Talam

Ingredients

For Bottom Layer:
1 kg (2.2Ib/35.2oz) pumpkin flesh - cut into 1 to 2 inch pieces
135 g (4.8 oz) rice flour
50 g (1.8 oz) tapioca flour
3 tablespoons agave syrup
2 teaspoons vanilla extract
160 ml coconut milk

For Top Layer:
100 g (3.5 oz) rice flour
50 g (1.8 oz) tapioca flour
100 g (3.5 oz) desiccated coconut
400 ml coconut milk
3 tablespoons agave syrup
1 teaspoons vanilla extract
1 cup (250 ml) water
1/4 teaspoon salt

Equipment:
8 inch deep square cake pan

Directions

Designed for Bottom Layer:
Warm-up a large wok half filled with water, make a large plate higher than a sizzling stand in the wok and add most the pumpkin items. Cover with cover and vapor upon medium warmth to get 10 moments or until virtually all the pumpkin items are soft. Remove dish make virtually all the pumpkins within a huge dish, mash well with a spud masher. In an additional huge bowl, blend the rice flour and tapioca flour with a beat. From then on add in the coconut dairy, agave syrup and vanilla extract, beat and mix well.

Intended for Bottom level Layer:
Adhere to with the aid of all the mashed pumpkin in to the flour combination in stage some. Whisk till virtually all the elements are well mixed. Collection the bottom level from the eight in. square wedding cake skillet with baking/parchment paper. Pour the pumpkin mixture in stage 4 in to the cake skillet. Warmth up the wok half complete of water once again, provide for a boil. Place the cake skillet on to the sizzling stand. Cover with cover and vapor upon medium warmth to get 25 moments.

To get top level level Layer:
Blend most of the grain flour, tapioca flour and desiccated coconut within a huge bowl, beat and mix well. After that add in most of the coconut milk, agave viscous, thick treacle, vanilla remove, drinking water and sodium. Beat all the elements together till well combined. Put the very greatest coating mixture on to the very finest of the ready pumpkin bottom covering in the wedding ceremony cake pan. Cover with lid and vapor for 30 moments. Be sure that right now there is certainly enough water in the wok. Awesome and refrigerate intended to get few hours or overnight before slicing.

28. Kuih Lopes (Coconut Glutinous Rice)

Ingredients

2 cups glutinous rice
Food coloring (typically green)
2 cups coconut milk
1/2 cup water
1 tsp pandan flavoring
1 tsp salt
fifteen tbs muscovado sugar and one cup of water
Grated coconut and some salt

Directions

Clean the rice and soak it with food coloring regarding 3 hours.
Drain water from materials and place materials inside rice oven along with coconut milk, water, salt and pandan flavor. Mix them well. Minus rice oven, just cook following the instructions after the rice product packaging. With grain oven, it is going to consider about half one hour.

This is the pandan flavoring All of us acquired from Malaysia. There's no option to the flavor, but easy to find in any sort of Asian market.

This is the coconut powder I utilize to create 2 mugs of coconut dairy.

While waiting around intended for the rice to prepare, make a glass of drinking drinking water to boil with muscovado sugar until it forms the density and nice taste you prefer. With this brand, All of us used 15 tablespoons. Allow it to cool.

When materials is completed, trim this within a sq. pan covered with baking paper. Be sure to flatten it, and let it amazing.

Cut into the sizes you choose and coat these grated coconut and sodium mixture. Provide with muscovado viscous, thick treacle that is ready previously.

29. Baked Spicy Stingray / Sambal Ikan Bakar

Ingredients

400 grams stingray or any fish
spicy sambal
2 kalamasi juice or lime juice
2 tbsp oil
1 small slice onion
1 tbsp light soy sauce
4 tbsp spicy sauce (sambal)

garnish
2 tbsp slice cucumbers
2 small kalamasi
1 small slice onion

Directions

In pan with gas saute spicy spices or herbs with onion designed for 1 minute and then add light soy bean sauce after that away heat.

Period well with sodium and pepper, after that place the stingray upon a clown keep, top prepared prepared spicy sambal along side onion after that close four part tightly and cook 200 C meant for twenty minute.

Drizzle Several Lime juice, red onion, cucumber and several fresh coriander leaves and provide.

30. Fifteen Minute LAKSA

Ingredients

5 Shallot
6 clove garlic
1 Thumb size piece of Ginger
2 tbsp Shrimp paste
1/2 cup water
2 1/2 cup chicken stock
12 Green Prawns
1/3 cup Laksa paste
400 ml Coconut Cream
8 Fish balls
1 tsp sugar
1 Splash of fish sauce
1 lime juice
1 Pack Vermicelli noodles
125 grams Shredded cooked chicken
1 coriander leaves and spring onions

Directions

Combine first 6 substances into a gentle paste. Shell prawns and fry addresses in 80 ml of oil relevant to 1 minute. Eliminate shells. Add mixed paste to essential oil And fry 1 minute, add 1/3 of laksa insert. Smolder until aromatic, add chicken share and bring to steam, Add coconut cream and simmer. Add fish golf golf balls, Sugar, fish spices or herbs and lime juice (or if you have to " lemon " juice) (or if you have to lemon juice) (or if you need to " " lemon " " juice) (or if you think you have to lemon juice).

Prepare vermicelli in skillet of hot water to drink, Scoop noodles into Colander, Poach prawns in same water to drink,

Transfer noodles and prawns to dish Ladle over broth, top with disposed cooked poultry and bean seedlings. Best with coriander leaves and sliced up springtime onions.

Printed in Great Britain
by Amazon

15833880R00043